Congratulations on a wonderful courageous and wonderful career of saving lives and property. I truly believe that God will bless you. You are making a decision to love and care for humanity in the time of emergencies.

A lot of people are suffering today whether it is homeless, not enough money, working too much just to pay bills. It's a stressful life.

As an African American Female Firefighter, I saw the relief on peoples face when I walked in their home or on scene. It was like here is someone who will help me. You will do the same no matter what nationality you are. People see women as caring individuals with a heart.

I have cried and prayed for so many people in my 21 year career. Lord Save them. Some will not make it and it will affect you mentally. It is a blessing to be in this world of firefighters.

Sandra Nelson

I dedicate this book to my sons Blake and Travis.

I only became a firefighter to give you the best life that I could as a Single Mother. Love you!

Photograph by Sandra Nelson
Last day working as a Firefighter
07/03/2017
I own the rights to this photo of me on my last day working on a fire in Illinois.

FLAMES OF RESILIENCE

BY: SANDRA NELSON

Copyright © 2023 Sandra Nelson

All rights reserved. No part of this book may be used or reproduced by any means, graphic, electronic, or mechanical, including photocopying, recording, taping or by any information storage retrieval system without the written permission of the author except in the case of brief quotations embodied in critical articles and reviews. A few examples or stories are from the author of this book (Retired Firefighter Sandra Nelson).

No part of this publication may be reproduced, distributed, or transmitted in any form or by any means, including photocopying, recording, or other electronic or mechanical methods, without the prior written permission or the publisher, except in the case of brief quotations embodied in reviews and certain other non commercial uses permitted by copyright law.

ISBN:
© Copyright 2023

TABLE OF CONTENTS

1	History of Female Firefighters	14
2	Female Firefighters Today	17
3	Example of Entry Exam	20
4	Things you never knew	24
5	Shift Bag Checklist	27
6	Woman's Hair	30
7	Physical Fitness	33
8	The Unlike Culture	35
9	Mindset	38
10	RESOURCES	46
11	Words of Encouragement	49
12	My Story	52

INTRODUCTION

Hello, my name is Sandra Nelson. I am glad you purchased my little book. I am a Retired Career Firefighter. Actually, I Retired as an Engineer. As I search the internet, I still see and read women's comments about the fire service.

So, I decided to write this book.

I hope this book gives you more insight of working as a Firefighter. I will list websites that you can get more information. There are so many things that I could talk about in my 21 years in the fire service. Some needs to be kept within me but a lot is worth telling you about being a woman in the fire service. Whether you are just beginning your career or you are inquiring about becoming a firefighter.

You have to know it is a hard and dangerous career. There are men on the department that plays different roles when accepting you as one of them. Some guys will accept you and help you succeed, some will not like you at all, some of them don't' care just don't get in their way, some are just mean and, some are misogynist (don't like women at all), some men are sneaky and show you the wrong way of doing things. You will know right away.

Embrace the men who are there willing to train you the right way to becoming the firefighter that you need to be. This career is dangerous so you here to save lives, property, and prevention. As women, people are watching your every move. People are watching to see if you are a real firefighter and that can you handle the job.

Remember: You are here to do a job, train to keep up on your skills and save lives. To be honest, I had a very hard time the first 14 years of my career. Now, my department had 5 women on the department when I was hired.

I tried to quit numerous times in my head but I was a Single mother with two sons. Around my 15th year, I moved up the ladder. Now I am in charge because of people leaving, retiring, left on disability etc. **I am an Engineer.**

I worked with another woman my entire career. We were friends and never got into a

disagreement. We continued to go to fire classes to stay current on the changing career.
Here are the ranks in the fire service.

- Probation Firefighter
- Firefighter
- Engineer
- Lieutenant
- Deputy Chief
- Fire Chief

NOTE: This is my department order in rank.

You must have to thick skin. Yes, it is alright to cry. I cried so much but they never knew it. That's the key! *Don't ever let them see you cry.*

I did a lot of praying and a lot of praying for people who we responded to on emergency calls.

WE ARE HUMAN!

Side Note: Firefighting is challenging and dangerous career that test you emotionally, physically, and mentally.

The Controversy

Women are entering the fire service at an alarming rate. Many people feel that inequality based on sex is natural, functional and in large measure unalterable. *(FEMA, 1998)*

The occupation of firefighter, like many others, is one that has traditionally been thought of as a man's job. *(Craig, 1985)*

As the department begins to include women, there are going to be some cultural diversity between men and women. Most men do not want to have the culture diversity training or sensitivity training. Men see this as a way to change their culture and tradition of the fire service. It is all about managing change aggressively and progressively. *(FEMA. 1998)*

Furthermore, the physical aspects of the job will always be an issue with women because it was known that women were the weaker sex when it comes to upper body strength.

Pro side of the controversy.

There is a new set of heroines. The heroines are women in the fire service. Women are breaking down barriers even if they know for a fact they are the unlike culture. Society views women in the fire service as a culture change and the approval of the job that you are doing.

The advantage of being a female firefighter is team work. In many fire departments hiring women, the men and women of a shift will spend 24 hours together in the same living quarters. *(Craig, 1985)*

Furthermore, women have to change their thinking in the male-environment as well. The National Fire Protection Association (NFPA) reports that there are 1,134,400 career and volunteer fire departments in the United States in which 82,550 (7%) are women. *(Hayes, 2016)*

While the statistics are low, more women are entering the field every year.

Con side of the controversy.

The fire service has its own culture and its rich with tradition and history. *(Hollenback III, 1985)* When women enter a field that is male-dominated, she must expect some kind of negative attitudes from her coworkers. *(Craig, 1985)*

The ongoing battle is that female firefighters have to constantly prove themselves even when they have advanced past the men. *(Hayes, 2016)* Men in the fire service have known this occupation as a tradition and culture of their own and it didn't include women. The culture is changing and it is a shock to men and society. It might be that women's roles are congruent with stereotypes due to physiological or cultural differences. *(Craig, 1985)*

Some men see women as a threat to the maleness of the organization. Some men generally see women as the weaker sex and that women do not have upper body strength. Women who pass are still represented at lower percentage than men, but they do pass. *(Hollenback III, (2014)* Some men cannot take this change and is so disturbed that they retaliate against women in a form of discrimination, harassment, and they create a hostile working environment.

While some cities are making progress by training and hiring women, but the job discrimination will persists with some departments. *(Craig, 1985)* *(ColumbiaSouthernUniversityEssaypaper2017)*

NOTES AND YOUR COMMENTS

Chapter 1

HISTORY OF FEMALE FIREFIGHTERS

Certainly! The history of female firefighters dates back to the early 19th century, although their presence in the fire service has been relatively recent compared to their male counterparts. Here is an overview of the history of female Firefighters:

Early Pioneers (1800s): In the 19th century, women began playing a role in firefighting. Some notable pioneers include:
Molly Williams, an African American slave who worked as a volunteer firefighter in New York City in the early 1800s, Yes, she was a slave in New York and was affiliated with the Ocean Engine Company #11 in 1818 *(Wikipedia) https://en.wikipedia.org/wiki/Molly_Williams*

She was a volunteer and her service was noted because it was during the blizzard of 1818. She wore a Calico dress and checked apron. She drags ropes and pulled the pumper to the fire through the deep snow *(Wikipedia) https://en.wikipedia.org/wiki/Molly_Williams*

World War II (1939-1945): During World War II, with many men serving in the military, women took on various roles traditionally held by men. This included serving as firefighters in both civilian and military capacities.

*The Women's Movement and Gender Equality (1960s-1970s): The women's rights movement in the 1960s and 1970s led to increased opportunities for women in previously male-dominated fields. Fire departments began to face pressure to open their ranks to women, leading to the gradual inclusion of female firefighters.

Milestone Moments: In the 1970s and 1980s, several significant milestones occurred in the integration of women into fire departments. These included the hiring of the first female career firefighter in the United States was Judith Livers Brewer. She became the first American Career Firefighter and the first American woman to serve as a Battalion Chief *(Wikipedia)*

Legal Challenges and Gender Discrimination: Women who sought careers in firefighting faced legal challenges and gender discrimination. Lawsuits were filed against fire departments, and court rulings helped establish equal opportunities for women in firefighting.

Over the years, the number of female firefighters has steadily increased. Fire departments around the world have implemented recruitment initiatives, mentorship programs, and diversity and inclusion policies to attract and retain female firefighters. However, women still face challenges related to gender bias, physical requirements, and limited representation in leadership positions.

Today, female firefighters play a vital role in firefighting and emergency response worldwide. They bring diverse skills, perspectives, and contributions to the profession. Efforts continue to be made to increase gender equality, provide supportive work environments, and celebrate the achievements of female firefighters.

It's important to note that the history of female firefighters can vary in different countries and regions, with progress occurring at different times and rates.

Chapter 2

FEMALE FIREFIGHTERS TODAY

According to Zippa.com, there are only 11.8% of women firefighters in the United States. The men average is 88.2%.

As of 2022, there are 25.813 firefighters working in the United States. So, we are still under as this is still an all male environment. Women firefighters work as Fire inspectors, Firefighters, Engineers, Lieutenants, Battalion Chiefs, Fire Chiefs, Volunteers, Wild land firefighters, Deputy Chiefs and Fire Commissioners.

According to *WomeninFire.com*, which started in 1982, the number of female firefighters was increasing but still not enough. Women in fire states there are about 150 district chiefs, battalion chiefs, assistant chiefs and division chiefs. This was in 1982. There is no data that is current for 2023 but we know it is a lot more.

Women firefighter can work in a variety of roles like Fire Secretary, Fire Inspectors, Arson

Investigators, Fire Chiefs, Deputy Chiefs, Division Chiefs, Wildland fires, and Volunteer firefighters which could be over 30,000 in the U.S.

Now, we can't leave out the large number of female firefighters that is overseas like Europe, Brazil, France, Japan, Canada etc.

So, you can see that women firefighter exist and the numbers are rising every year.

These websites can provide resources, support, and information specifically tailored to female firefighters:

Women in Fire (www.womeninfire.org) a non-profit organization dedicated to supporting and empowering women in the fire service. Their website offers resources, networking opportunities, mentorship programs, information on conferences and events.

International Association of Women in Fire & Emergency Services (www.i-women.org). It is an international organization focused on advancing women in the fire services and emergency services. Their website provides resources, educational opportunities, leadership developments and network.

FirefighterCloseCalls.com (www.firefigher-closecalls.com) this website has valuable information on firefighter safety, incident reports, lessons learned, and up to date news.

Firehouse.com Women Firefighters (www.firehouse.com/women) a leading online resource for the fire service community. It has a section dedicated for women firefighters. News, articles, videos and discussions open to women in the fire service.

United Women Firefighters (www.unitedwomenfirefighters.org) is an organization based in New York City that advocates for the inclusion and advancement of women in the fire service. The website provides information on training programs, events and resources.

Federal Emergency Management Agency (1993) "The Changing Face of the Fire Service".

Chapter 3

ENTRY LEVEL TESTING

Together with IAFF (International Association of Firefighter) and International Fire Chief Association Joint Labor-Management Candidate Physical Ability Test, consist of 8 separate events to perform and the time must be under 10:20 or less.

THIS IS A PASS/FAIL TEST!

What are the steps of CPAT test when applying for the fire service?

CPAT (Candidate Physical Ability Test) is a standardized physical fitness test commonly used in the fire service hiring process. While specific test formats may vary between jurisdictions or states but here are the general steps involved in the CPAT:

Introduction and Orientation: Candidates are provided with an overview of the CPAT test, including the tasks they will be required to complete and the safety protocols to follow.

Stair Climb: must wear a weighted vest (usually 50 pounds) and additional 25lbs or climb a set of stairs maybe in full gear/air pack/etc

Hose Drag: Candidates are required to drag a charged hose line for a specified distance (usually 75 feet) while maintaining control and keeping a steady pace. This part of test can be pulling a hose line from an apparatus or in a building with obstacles like around corners etc. Put the hose line over your shoulder.

Equipment Carry: Candidates must pick up various firefighting equipment (such as chainsaw, sledgehammer, K12 saw) and carry them for a set distance (usually 75 feet) while maintaining balance and control.

Ladder Raise and Extension: Candidates are tasked with extending a ladder by raising it from a horizontal position to a vertical position. The ladder used in the test is typically a 24-foot extension ladder. You might have to lower and raise a ladder and hand over hand to raise the ladder.

Forcible Entry: Candidates simulate the action of forcibly opening a door by using a sledgehammer to strike a designated target. Don't drop the sledgehammer

Rescue Drag: Candidates must drag a mannequin weighing approximately 65-200 pounds for a set distance (usually 35 feet) to simulate rescuing a victim. Crawling on your hands and knees through a narrow portion.

Search and Rescue: Candidates navigate through a designated maze while wearing a self-contained breathing apparatus (SCBA) usually 35 feet to simulate rescuing or removing a victim. It might have a 165lb mannequin and have to drag it to the finish line.

Ceiling Breach/Pull: the Candidate fully pushes up the hinged door in the ceiling with the pike pole 3 times. The candidate then hooks the pike pole to the ceiling device and pulls the pole down 5 times.

(Please note every department has different requirements)

It's important to note that these steps are a general overview of the CPAT test, and the specific details and requirements may vary depending on the fire department or jurisdiction conducting the test. It is recommended to check with the fire department you are applying to for the most accurate and up-to-date information regarding their CPAT.

Look at these you tube videos:

- CPAT Test: Pass the Firefighter CPAT test
- Firefighter CPAT test in 6:45
- Firefighter CPAT test Walkthrough
- CPAT Orientation
- CPAT Candidate Walkthrough
- 114 lb Female Candidate Demonstrates how to pass the test
How to pass the test

You have a written exam, physical ability test, Medical Examination, Psychological Evaluation, Background Check, and Oral Interview.

Please note: These entry level testing could be different for Wild land Firefighters/Paid on Call/Part time. Please check with your local fire department that you are interested in to start your career.

Chapter 4

Things No one told you about Being a Female Firefighter

You can be just as capable and successful as your male counterparts; Gender does not determine your firefighting abilities. The fire service is gradually becoming more inclusive and diverse, but you may still encounter stereotypes and bias from some individuals.

Physical fitness is crucial for firefighting, so regular exercise and strength training is important to prepare for the demands of the job. Protective gear, such as turnout gear and breathing apparatus, may not always fit perfectly, but there are options available to ensure proper fit for women.

The fire service is a male-dominated field, and you may find yourself being the only woman in your department. This can be both challenging and rewarding. It is essential to find a support network within the fire service, whether it's other female firefighters, mentors, online support groups, online social media who can provide guidance and encouragement.

You may face unique challenges related to personal hygiene and privacy, such as finding appropriate facilities for changing and dealing with long hair.

Balancing work and personal life can be demanding, particularly if you have family responsibilities and your relationships with your significant other.

Be prepared for skepticism and doubt from the public, especially when responding to emergencies. Show confidence in your abilities and let your actions speak for themselves. You may need to prove yourself repeatedly again and again to gain respect and recognition. Don't be discourage by setbacks, and continue to demonstrate your skills 110%.

The job can be emotionally and mentally challenging, with exposure to traumatic situations. Seek support and debriefing resources to process these experiences.

Engage in continuous learning and training to stay updated with the latest firefighting techniques and safety procedures. Always keep your head in fire books and laws about the fire service. Each state is different but similar in regards to staying safe and saving lives.

Please note: A lot of departments require you to be a Paramedic or EMT (Emergency Medical Technician) so you will have to go to class, pass the class and get your state licensed. The State test is hard but you can pass it.

Your skills and contributions extend beyond firefighting. Consider opportunities in fire investigation, fire inspector/prevention, education, and leadership roles.

Take care of your mental and physical well-being. Engage in self care practices to prevent burnout and promote a good work like balance.

You can make a significant impact in your community as a firefighter. Embrace the opportunity to service and protect others, and always be proud of your chosen profession.

Chapter 5

SHIFT BAG CHECKLIST

As a female firefighter, you want to make sure you have everything you need to work 24, 48, or 72 hour shift. As women, we need a lot of stuff. I looked at shift work like going on vacation.

When I reported for Duty, I had a huge suitcase, backpack, computer etc.

Here is a breakdown of what I brought:

CLOTHES

- Extra Clothes
- Pants, Fire Class B Pants or EMS Pants
- Socks
- (2 T Shirts)
- Shoes- one gym shoes and hard men's work boots
- Slippers after shower
- Sports Bras- ones you don't like
- 3 pks of Underwear
- Long Johns for winter
- Comforter, Sheets, and my own pillow

WASHROOM ITEMS

- Lotion
- Shower Gel/Soap
- Feminine Napkins/Tampons– have extra
- Bath towels– get at the Dollar store
- Washcloths–get at the Dollar store
- Hair Shampoo and Conditioner
- Curling Iron or Blow Dryer
- Rubber bands
- Hair ties
- Comb, Brush, Hair pins
- Foundation—I only used a little
- Nail File and Nail Cutter for hang nails
- Wash Scrub to get the dirt off

YOUR MEDICAL BAG

- Band aids
- Alcohol pads
- Tissue—small box will last a long time
- Your medications
- Over the Counter, Diarrhea, Pain meds, Tums, Aspirin, Vitamins. Pain spray if needed

SIDE NOTE: *When you come home from work, take the clothes that you wore off at the door and put in your washing machine. Or you can do this at the fire station and change. But always remember check with your Lieutenant or check the Rules and Regulations.*

Most of the items, you will just keep in a small bag and never touch them. You will not need them every day so leave it in your suitcase.

I bring everything on this list. You can keep this suitcase in the trunk of the car. No one will see the contents of your bag but you.

It is best to be prepared for anything as working in an all male environment.

Very important:

ALWAYS BRING YOUR FIRE BOOKS TO LEARN ABOUT BECOMING A FIREFIGHTER AND STUDYING FOR STATE FIRE TEST.

YOU WILL BE TAKING CLASSES AND STUDYING FOR CLASSES YOUR ENTIRE CAREER IF YOU WANT TO MOVE UP THE LADDER. ALWAYS BE ON TOP OF YOUR GAME. WE HAVE TO WORK 110%.

Chapter 6

Women's Hair

When working as a female firefighter, it's important to prioritize safety and ensure that your hair is properly managed to prevent any hazards or interference during firefighting operations.

First, secure ponytail or braid: Tie your hair back in a secure ponytail or braid to keep it away from your face and reduce the risk of it getting caught on equipment or obstructing your vision.

Bun or low-profile hairstyle, if your hair is long enough to create a bun that sits close to your head. This keeps your hair contained and reduces the chances of it interfering with your protective gear.

Experiment with hairstyles that work well with your firefighting helmet. Protective head gear or wearing a bandana under your helmet can absorb sweat and keep your hair in place. This additional layer can help prevent hair from obstructing your vision or causing discomfort during long shifts.

Removing the smell of smoke from your hair can be challenging, but here are some ideas to help mitigate and eliminate the odor:

- Wash your hair thoroughly and use a good quality shampoo designed to eliminate strong odors. Be sure to lather you hair well, focusing on the roots and scalp.

- After shampooing, rinse your hair with a mixture of equal parts water and white vinegar. The acidic properties of vinegar can help neutralize and eliminate odors. Rinse your half again with plain water. Please check with your stylist before using vinegar.

- Create a paste by mixing baking soda with water. Apply the past to your hair and let it sit for 10-15 minutes before rinsing it out. Baking soda can help absorb and neutralize odors.

- Add a few drops of your preferred essential oil to a spray bottle filled with water. Spritz your hair lightly to help mask any lingering odors. Choose oils with strong scents like lavender, peppermint, or citrus. (Please check with you hairstylist or doctor before trying).

- Dry shampoo can help absorb oils and odors in your hair. Apply a dry shampoo specifically, formulated for odor elimination and follow the product instructions.

CHECK WITH YOUR DEPARTMENT FOR SPECIFIC HAIR REGULATIONS OR GUIDLINES

If the smoke smell persists, consider visiting a professional hair salon. They may have specialized treatments or techniques to help remove stubborn odors from your hair.

Remember, the effectiveness of these methods may vary depending on the intensity and duration of smoke exposure. It may take a few attempts or combination of methods to completely eliminate the odor. Find what works for you.

Chapter 7

Physical Fitness

As a female firefighter, maintaining a physical fitness is crucial for advancing in the fire service.

Cardiovascular exercise will elevate your heart rate and improve cardiovascular endurance. This includes running, cycling, swimming, or using treadmills or elliptical. Aim for at least 30 minutes of moderate to vigorous aerobic exercise, three to five times a week.

Incorporate resistance training exercises to build overall strength and functional fitness. Focus on movement that works with the muscle groups including squats, jumping, dead lifts, bench presses, and overhead presses.

Core exercises strengthening are crucial for stability and injury prevention such as planks, leg raises, and crunches. Try and target your lower back muscles, abdominal, and oblique's.

Firefighting often involves burst of intense activity followed by rest periods.

Firefighters must have good balance and coordination. Incorporate exercises such as single-leg exercises, single leg squats, and single leg dead lifts, balance board or ladder drills.

Endurance training can develop muscular endurance by incorporating exercises that require prolonged effort, such as step-ups, lunges or stair climbing.

These exercises will help you build the stamina needed for extended periods of physical exertion.

Remember to consult with a healthcare professional or certified fitness trainer before starting any new exercise program. They can provide guidance based on your individual needs and ensure proper form and technique.

NOTE: I joined a gym and did some workouts at home. The last 5 years my back was hurting so I had to stop going to the gym but was able to do some of the exercises I mentioned here. During my 15th year, I was promoted to Engineer.

Chapter 8

UNLIKE CULTURE

Throughout history, men have dominated many occupations because of cultural views and the division of labor determined by societies needs. *(Hollenback III.2014)*

Long ago, these male jobs have excluded women from many occupations such as firefighting and police officer for a variety of reasons. As you can read history, women weren't even able to work, their paychecks went to their husbands, and women could not vote or speak out. Over the years, the strategy has been to increase the presence of women in the fire service. Statistics is still lower in the fire service because of exclusionary culture still exists *(Hollenback III.2014)*.

According to *Hollenback III*, the reasons for the lower numbers of women in the fire service have been examined by discrimination and physiology. But, it is a known fact for the lower numbers is the lack of desire and weaker physiology *(Hollenback III. 2014)*

Female firefighters are unlike any other culture in the fire service and around the world.

To all my aspiring female firefighters and firefighters, you must keep your head up, push through it because if I can do it, so can you. Female firefighters are fighting for a place in the fire service. There are so many occupations in the fire service besides fire suppression.

Where have been excluded because it is seen as "man's domain," when that society needs bodies in an emergency, gender is not a disqualifier, only an identifier.
Do you know how many people in my community saw me with the firefighters and said Congratulations or you go girl you are doing it. Others just stare at you to see if you know what you are doing.

SHORT STORY

We had only 3 firefighter working this day and it happened to be 3 of us women. Oh boy, did the men was not happy but the Chief states "It is what it is". We had a car fire on a highway and had to pull a guy out of the vehicle. He stated to the Fire Chief, your men did an awesome job and Thank you!

The Fire Chief told him "those are the women on the department. The EMS crew that responded was women too. He said he couldn't believe that all who responded for his emergency was women.

So, the Fire Chief had us come over and told us to take off our helmets and the man was in Awe. He said he will never doubt women again because he thought he was going to die in that car. Praise God is ok just some burns but nothing serious.

So, see how women can change a person thinking of women in the fire service or Emergency Medical Technicians.

Check out where you live and see if there is training and/or academy to train women as firefighters. I heard that New York had an academy for women to become New York Firefighters but don't quote me on that.

Chapter 9

MINDSET

What could a woman firefighter mindset be in the fire service?

A woman firefighter's mindset in the fire service can vary from individual to individual. However, here are some common elements that may contribute to a woman firefighter's mindset:

Confidence:
Believe in your abilities and know that you are capable of handling the challenges of firefighting.

Determination:
Be Resilient and persistent in pursuing your firefighting career goals. From Cadet to Fire Chief

Courage:
Embrace bravery in the face of danger and uncertainty.

Physical Fitness:
Prioritize your health and maintain a high level of physical fitness to meet the demands of firefighting.

Mental Toughness:
Develop mental resilience to handle stressful and intense situations of the job.

Team Player:
Collaborate effectively with fellow firefighters and value the importance of teamwork. Collaborate with other female firefighters on other fire departments.

Continuous Learning:
Always be open to learning and improving your skills and knowledge.

Adaptability:
Be flexible and able to adjust to various scenarios and changing conditions.

Self-Reliance:
Be Self-sufficient and capable of handling tasks Independently.

Problem-Solving Skills:

Develop strong problem-solving abilities to make quick and critical decisions during emergencies.

Empathy:
Show Compassion and understanding towards victims and fellow team members.

Effective Communication:
Develop clear and concise communication skills for efficient teamwork and public interactions.

Respect:
Respect the diverse perspectives and backgrounds of your colleagues and the community you serve.

Positive Attitude:
Maintain a positive outlook even in challenging situations.

Safety Consciousness:
Prioritize safety for yourself and others at all times.

Calm under Pressure:
Keep your composure during emergencies and high-stress situations.

Leadership Skills:
Cultivate leadership qualities to take charge when necessary and inspire others.

Humility:
Acknowledge your strengths and weaknesses, and always be willing to learn from others.

Focus on Service:
Remember that firefighting is a service-oriented profession aimed at protecting and assisting the community.

Perseverance:
Stay committed to your firefighting career and the positive impact you can make in people's lives.

By adopting these mindsets, women firefighters can excel in their roles and contribute significantly to the fire service in the United States. The fire service benefits from diversity and women bring unique perspectives and strengths that enrich the profession as a whole.

Competence and Capability:
Women firefighters often strive to establish themselves as competent and capable professionals in their field. They approach their work with a mindset of skill development, continuous learning, and mastery of firefighting techniques.

Resilience and Determination:
Firefighting can be physically and emotionally demanding, and a woman firefighter's mindset often includes resilience and determination. They embrace challenges, overcome obstacles, and maintain a positive attitude in the face of adversity.

Teamwork and Collaboration:
Women firefighters recognize the importance of teamwork and collaboration in their profession. They value the collective efforts of their colleagues and understand that effective teamwork is essential for successful firefighting operations.

Breaking Stereotypes and Inspiring Others:
Many women firefighters are motivated by the desire to break gender stereotypes and inspire other women to pursue careers in firefighting. They approach their work with a sense of purpose and see themselves as role models for future generations.

Adaptability and Flexibility:
Firefighters need to be adaptable and flexible in dynamic and rapidly changing situations. Women firefighters embrace this mindset, recognizing the need to quickly adjust their approach and tactics to effectively respond to emergencies.

Service and Community Focus:
A woman firefighter's mindset often includes a strong sense of service and commitment to the community. They view firefighting as a noble profession and take pride in protecting and serving others.

Lifelong Learning and Professional Growth:
Women firefighters understand the importance of continuous learning and professional growth.

They actively seek out training opportunities, stay undated on industry developments, and strive for personal and career advancement.

Safety and Risk Management:
Safety is a priority for women firefighters. They approach their work with a mindset of risk assessment, adherence to safety protocols, and ensuring the well-being of themselves and their team member.

Empathy and Compassion:
Women firefighters bring empathy and compassion to their work. They understand the human element involved in firefighting, such as providing support to victims, displaying empathy towards those affected by emergencies, and offering emotional support to their colleagues.

Confidence and Self-Belief:
Women Firefighters cultivate confidence and self-brief in their abilities. They trust their training, experience, and skills, allowing them to perform their duties effectively and make critical decisions under pressure.

It's important to note that these aspects of a woman firefighter's mindset are not exclusive to them and can also be shared by their male counterparts. Firefighters, regardless of gender often possess similar values and perspectives when it comes to their profession.

Chapter 10

RESOURCES

Here is a list of some government organizations and agencies that may support or be related to women in firefighting.

United States

U.S. Fire Administration (USFA): provides resources and training for firefighters in general.

International Association of Women in Fire & Emergency Services (iWomen): A nonprofit organization that supports women in the fire and emergency services field.

International Association of Fire Chiefs (IAFC): The IAFC represents the leadership of fire and emergency service organizations throughout the world. While not focused solely on women, it addresses various issues affecting firefighters.

State and Local Firefighter Associations: Many states and localities have firefighter associations that may offer support and resources for women firefighters. Examples include the California Fire

Chiefs Association, and the New York State Association of Fire Chiefs.

Federal and State Employment Agencies: Federal and state employment agencies may have resources and information about job opportunities and support for women in firefighting.

United Kingdom:
Women in the Fire Service UK: An organization dedicated to supporting and promoting women in the UK fire and rescue services.

Canada:
Women in Firefighting Canada: An organization that promotes the recruitment and advancement of women in firefighting and emergency services in Canada.

India:
Women in Fire Services India: An imitative aimed at promoting gender diversity and equality within the Indian fire services.

South Africa:
Women in Fire and Emergency (WIFES): A network that supports empowers women in the fire and emergency services in South Africa.

Every state should have a peer support organization where firefighter's men and women can talk to them and get some insight on how to maintain your mindset. This organization or others will come and talk to the crew after a death or bad call. Its Called PEER SUPPORT. Check your local area or state.

Chapter 11

WORDS OF ENCOURGMENT
ASIRING TO BECOME A FIREFIGHTER

Embarking on a journey as a woman in the fire service is a courageous and empowering decision that holds the potential to inspire countless others. Your determination to break barriers and embrace a traditionally male-dominated field is a testament to your strength and resilience. Remember that every step you take paves the way for progress, and your presence will undoubtedly contribute to a more diverse and inclusive firefighting community.

In the face of challenges, draw strength from the knowledge that your skills, passion and dedication are what truly define you as a firefighter. Your unique perspective and abilities have the power to enrich the entire firefighting team, fostering innovation and fresh approaches to problem-solving. Embrace each hurdle as an example for others but will also play an essential role in ensuring the safety and well-being of your community.

As you step into the fire service, keep your focus on your aspirations and the positive impact you can create. Surround yourself with mentors and allies who support your journey and share your vision for a more inclusive and diverse firefighting world. Your presence matters, your contributions are invaluable, and your dedication is an inspiration to us all. Embrace the challenges, stand tall in the face of adversity, and continue to blaze a train that will light the way for future generations of women in the fire service.

WORDS FOR ENCOURGMENT FOR WOMEN WHO ARE WORKING FIREFIGHTERS

To the remarkable women who are already blazing trails as firefighters, your unwavering commitment and dedication to serve as a beacon for all. Every day you step into the fire station you are making history for all the young women who wants to become a firefighter. You challenge stereotypes and prove that courage knows no gender. Your resilience in the face of adversity and unyielding excellence is testaments to your remarkable strength.

In the demanding and high stakes world of firefighting, your skills and leadership are driving forces that will elevate your team. As you continue, to overcome obstacles and shatter glass ceilings, your achievements are making waves far beyond the fire station doors. Your dedication and strength is so important and Society is watching you as a firefighter.

Your dedication to this noble profession services as a source of pride and empowerment for countless individuals who look up to your with admiration. Keep pushing boundaries, keep nurturing your growth, stay updated with the latest state qualifications/testing.

Keep igniting the flames of progress as a trailblazer and role model for generations to come.

CHAPTER 12

MY STORY

As a retired firefighter, I just want to let women know that you can become a firefighter. Yes, it is so hard. I moved back home to be with my dad with 2 small sons while getting divorced. They were 2 and 4 years old. As we was coming back home from eating dinner, I saw an Ambulance coming down the street and told my dad that I want to work on the ambulance.

I wanted to be a Radiologist but the waiting list at a lot of colleges in my area was 7 years. So, I enrolled into a local college for Emergency Medical Technician. In the 3rd quarter, we had to get fire gear and connect with a fire department to learn how to extricate patients from vehicles. So, I asked my dad if he knew anyone.

He talked to his barber and he stated that a childhood friend he knew is a Deputy Fire Chief in the same town that we grew up as a child. So, I contacted him and he got me some fire gear.

As I was talking to him, he mentioned that I could become a firefighter. I laughed. I said "They are not going to hire me because I am a woman". He said "that is not true". We have 5 women on the department and if they can do it so can you. I graduated from EMT School. About 6 months later, the fire department was hiring. So, I submitted my application.

The hiring test consists of an Application, Physical Agility, Oral, Physic test and passing a criminal background. It was extremely hard. I had to run
1.5 miles at a certain time, pushups, running us stairs with preconnect hose, climbing up an aerial ladder, etc. But I did it. **NOTE: After taking the Physical test, I couldn't walk for 3 days**.

When the final lineup came out, I was 7th on the list. So, a year later, they called me and I started working in 1996. I just couldn't believe that I made it.

One firefighter said to me that I don't belong here. I didn't say anything to him because I was on probation. Probation was 18 months long. Other guys accepted me but they thought I paid my way into the department. My father had money but not like that. He was retired. Other guys didn't like me at all. The department was made up of Caucasians, African American, and Hispanic. The women were 2 African American, and 3 Caucasians.

When I joined the fire department, I was working part time as an EMT and a waitress. So, I quit those jobs to work full time at the fire department. They never sent me to the fire academy and had to train on the job. About a year later, I wrote a to-from to the Fire Chief stating that he must send me to the fire academy because I am not learning a lot working here. He decided and they sent me and another guy the academy. I was the only African American Woman and the other firefighter was African American too. I still have that photo. We studied on shift and talked on the phone trying to pass these fire classes.

While I was in the academy and EMT-I school, the Fire Chief tried to fire us because we was not State Certified Firefighters. It was crazy. So, my father contacted a lawyer to sue because we are passing the academy and EMT-I school. Yes, they sent us to the academy and EMT school at the same time for us to fail. It was hard but we passed and that lawsuit went away. He didn't' have a leg to stand on.

Believe me there was a lot of tears. I was trying to quit and find other jobs but some of the women and men said to me 'Don't quit!" That is what they want and don't give it to them.

About a year later, my dad had a heart attack while I was working. The lieutenant that day said to me we are going over there. So, we took my dad to the hospital and he called the Chief and told him that I am not coming back to shift. He tried to fire me for leaving shift. When it reached the Mayor, the Mayor said "No, you will not fire her because her dad had a heart attack and he almost died". The Mayor said we are in the business of saving lives and that includes family. Thank God he made it.

About 6 years later, I started taking classes and the Engineer test. I passed the Engineer test. In 2009, I got my Fire Science AA degree. So, after the 13th year, I made Engineer and some days I was Acting Lieutenant. WOOHOO!

Now, there was more pressure on me to lead the department and be Incident Commander.

What happened to the 6 Women on the department?

1. Sadly one passed away.
2. One left the department moved to Arizona
3. One left to work at the railroad and get her degree.
4. One quit it was too much
5. **One was still there**
6. **I was still there**

It came down to me and another female firefighter. So, we had to stick together. We went to classes together and kept in constant communications with each other. We never had an argument because we knew that we had to prove ourselves in the firefighter world. We moved up the ranks. I retired before her as an Engineer. She retired as a Lieutenant.

I was next in line for Lieutenant but I couldn't do it anymore. My body was breaking down from all the heavy gear and work. Mentally, I was just tired of it. So, I retired after 21 years.

One thing that did help me throughout my career was that I had an African American Fire Chief, Deputy Chief, and African American Mayor. It wasn't a smooth ride but I was hired as a Firefighter to save lives, protect property, and save lives in medical emergencies.

It is a rewarding career.

1. Did I have challenges? **YES**
2. Did I keep a log of what happened to me every shift for years and what was said to me? **YES**
3. Did I see therapy during my fire career? **YES**
4. Did I want to quit numerous times? **YES**
5. Did a cry a lot and was in pain? **YES**
6. Did I doubt myself? **YES**
7. Did I stay by myself because of the situation in the fire house? **YES**

8. Did a Lieutenant not speak to me for 2 years because he just didn't want too or something I said or Did?
YES
9. Did I study the fire books? **YES**

It's important to note that individuals' opinions and attitudes can vary widely, and it would be inaccurate to make generalizations about how all men feel about women in the fire service. However, I can provide some insights based on common perspectives and experiences.

In many cases, men in the fire service care supportive and welcoming of women firefighters. They recognize that gender does not determine one's ability to perform the job effectively. Many men appreciate the diverse perspectives and skills that women bring to the team. They value the qualities of dedication, teamwork, and professionalism demonstrated by their female colleagues.

That being said, there may be some men who hold biases or preconceived notions about women in traditionally male-dominated professions like firefighting. These individuals may have concerns about physical capabilities, perceived preferential treatment, or potential disruptions to the team dynamic.

However, it is crucial to understand that these opinions do not reflect the views of all men in the fire service. Overtime, more women join and excel in firefighting roles, stereotypes and biases tend to diminish. Increased representation and awareness have helped foster a more inclusive and accepting environment within the fire service. Efforts to educate and promote gender equality have been instrumental in challenging and changing outdated attitudes.

Ultimately, the attitudes of men towards women in the fire service can vary from person to person. However, it is essential to focus on promoting inclusivity, mutual respect, and equal opportunities for all firefighters, regardless of their gender.

Ladies, therapy is good if you are going through a lot. I was a Single mother of two kids, working at the fire department.

.

I hope this book helps you succeed in your career as a firefighter whether you are volunteer, career or paid on call. I wish you all luck and prayers in your career. Keep your head up and make us retired female firefighters proud.

This book is only for self help and determination if you want to be a female firefighter.

Sandra Nelson

Printed in the United States..
This is a work of nonfiction. All of the events in this book or stories are my stories and they are true in fact. This author is no way representing any company, fire department, corporation, or brand mentioned herein. The views expressed in this collection are solely those of the author. All information can be access on the internet. The conversations or actions in this book all come from the author's recollections. Rather, the author has retold them in a way that evokes the feelings and meaning what was said and in all instances, the essence of the dialogue is accurate. This book is not to discourage anyone from learning about the fire service. These are facts. Not every fire department in the U.S. will have any issues but you must be aware and informed.

REFERENCES

Craig, J.M., R. R. (1985)
Hayes 2016 & 2012
Hollenback III, D.R. (2014) & (2016)
Federal Emergency Management Agency (1998)

Federal Emergency Management Agency (1993)
(The Changing Face of the Fire Service)

www.firefighterclosecalls.com/women

www.i-woman.org

Milestone Moments: 1970-1980
Integration of Women into Fire Department

National Fire Protection Agency

National Testing:
www.nationaltestingnetwork.com/FAQ
CPAT Testing- www.youtube.com
Firefighter close calls: www.firefighterclosecalls.com

www.Unitedwomanfirefighter.org
Wikipedia: www.wikipedia.com/MollyWilliams
And www.wikipedia.com/Milestonemoments
World War II (1939-1945) Women Firefighters

www.Zippa.com –percentage of female and male firefighters

www.Firehouse.com
https://womeninfire.org

NFPA– National Fire Protection Association
www.nfpa.org – % of women and men

FEMA– "Book the Changing Face of the Fire Service Handbook–2012 (11 years ago)

This book is not to deter anyone or any fire department or fire protection districts from applying to become a Female Firefighter. All information in this book was noted and I personally know about the information in this book from working 21 years on a fire department.

This book doesn't tell all the information. It is a self-help book for women who want a Career as a Firefighter. Some parts of this book comes from personal knowledge and some extensive research of existing websites. Every State and local Fire Departments will have their own Rules and Regulations, State Laws, and information for the public. Don't take it personally!

Sandra Nelson

Printed in Great Britain
by Amazon